THE SWEET ENIGMA OF IT ALL

other books by the author

POETRY
Dawn Visions
Burnt Heart/Ode to the War Dead
This Body of Black Light Gone Through the Diamond
The Desert is the Only Way Out
The Chronicles of Akhira
The Blind Beekeeper
Mars & Beyond
Laughing Buddha Weeping Sufi
Salt Prayers
Ramadan Sonnets
Psalms for the Brokenhearted
I Imagine a Lion
Coattails of the Saint
Abdallah Jones and the Disappearing-Dust Caper (illustrated by the author)
Love is a Letter Burning in a High Wind
The Flame of Transformation Turns to Light
Underwater Galaxies
The Music Space
Cooked Oranges
Through Rose Colored Glasses
Like When You Wave at a Train and the Train Hoots Back at You
In the Realm of Neither
The Fire Eater's Lunchbreak
Millennial Prognostications
You Open a Door and it's a Starry Night
Where Death Goes
Shaking the Quicksilver Pool
The Perfect Orchestra
Sparrow on the Prophet's Tomb
A Maddening Disregard for the Passage of Time
Stretched Out on Amethysts
Invention of the Wheel
Sparks Off the Main Strike
Chants for the Beauty Feast
In Constant Incandescence
Holiday from the Perfect Crime
The Caged Bear Spies the Angel
The Puzzle
Ramadan is Burnished Sunlight
Ala-udeen & The Magic Lamp (illustrated by the author)
The Crown of Creation (illustrated by the author)
Blood Songs
Down at the Deep End (with drawings by the author)
Next Life
A Hundred Little 3D Pictures
He Comes Running
The Throne Perpendicular to all that is Horizontal
The Soul's Home
Eternity Shimmers / Time Holds its Breath
Stories Too Fiery to Sing Too Watery to Whisp;er
The Sweet Enigma of it All

THEATER / THE FLOATING LOTUS MAGIC OPERA COMPANY
The Walls Are Running Blood
Bliss Apocalypse

the sweet enigma of it all

poems

January 29 – June 18, 2014

Daniel Abdal-Hayy Moore

The Ecstatic Exchange
2014
Philadelphia

The Sweet Enigma of it All

Printed in the United States of America

The Ecstatic Exchange,
6470 Morris Park Road, Philadelphia, PA 19151-2403
email: abdalhayy@danielmoorepoetry.com

First Edition
ISBN: 978-0-578-15511-1 (paper)
Published by *The Ecstatic Exchange,*
6470 Morris Park Road, Philadelphia, PA 19151-2403

Cover art by the author
Book design by the author
Back cover photograph by the author (in Fez, Morocco).
Calligraphy by Haji Noor Deen Mi Guang Jiang

DEDICATION

To

Shaykh ibn al-Habib

(and the continuation of the Habibiyya)

Shaykh Bawa Muhaiyuddeen,

all shuyukh of instruction and ma'arifa,

Baji Tayyaba Khanum

of the unsounded depths,

Doctor Peter Prociuk, healer and Godsend,

&

blessed wife Malika, at my side,

al-hamdulillah,

The earth is not bereft

of Light

CONTENTS

INTRODUCTION

We're always at a crossroads. We may be in motion, we may be sitting still, we may be at peace or confronted with crisis. Even what to eat next puts us in the realm of choice and decision. And our approach to what road to take is part of our spiritual reservoir, our capacity for both determination and submission to whatever outcome God uses to reward our decision, our choice perhaps far from inspired or God-directed, but leading always to a divinely decided end (as well as — *in reality* — its beginning). This fact should make Sufis of us all. God's Way the Path of least resistance when our Fate is concerned, with faith that such "handing over the management of our affairs" (as the great shaykh, Ibn 'Ata-'Illah, titled one of his masterworks) will result in an illumined consequence, however cheerfully or difficult such an attitude may be to maintain. But I've been in the company of truly devout saintly ones, who take all their directives from The Source, from Allah, each moment, and wait for signs and confirmations before making any actions, major or minor. And they are not mad, and they are not deluded. They are illuminated and completely tranquil in their patience and in their place. And in their moment. Completely at ease in the eternal present.

What is it that so tranquilizes them, when at any moment a life or death decision may confront them, and yet they sail on calm waters throughout? What is this serene certainty that doesn't stop them in their tracks, but liberates them into wider and wider dimensions, some of them Unseen? How can death itself seem to them such a trifle, some discomfort to put up with but to be embraced, not as fanatics, but from pinnacles of wisdom, snowy peaks with a sunlight flash directly on them? Or really Allah's Light drawing them on in all sweetness? O magnet of impossibliity that pulls us forward through all our impossible obstacles! Magnet of bliss with its promises and actualities! Allah the Merciful...

During the writing of these poems I was diagnosed with stage four cancer, given about a year or so from a mainstream oncologist, strove submissively and manfully through initial five chemotherapies that were total torture, and chose to stop further doses in favor of a Sufi brother's professional alternative to build up rather than sap the strength of my own natural immune system, using holistic methods of wheat grass and strong hemp oil, which gave me many months of gentle joy. Even without unconditional success so far, I stand by this choice. (In the morning of my last PET scan I heard a voice say to me directly: *You shall be blessed.*) These poems chart the inspiratons of this time. I've taken the sweeter medicine, with a core axis of certainty in the Absolute Godly Promise, via His beloved Prophet Muhammad, may Allah's blessing be upon him. And as we say, *all success is with Allah.* He is Sufficient for us, and the best of Protectors.

1/14/15

"Do not curse time, for time is Allah

— Hadith of the Prophet Muhammad *(salallahu alayhi wa sallam)*

...Because... time is inexorable

— Faqir Shakir Masoud

Like a drunk sergeant, death stalks about the house
Kicking the furniture

— Eamon Grennan, Irish poet, playwright

"But as for the senile ones who believed and were righteous, because of their obedience and patience with senility and old age, and their having surmounted the difficulties and bore the burdens of worship, their reward is uninterrupted. Anas reported that the Prophet said, 'When the believer reaches fifty years of age, Allah lightens his account; when he reaches sixty, Allah grants him penitence; when he reaches seventy, he is loved by the inhabitants of the heavens; when he reaches eighty, righteous deeds are recorded for him and Allah pardons his misdeeds; when he reaches ninety, his sins are forgiven, he is allowed to intercede for his household, and he is Allah's prisoner on earth; and when he reaches one hundred and is unable to perform (righteous) works, he will have written for him all of the righteous works he used to perform during his period of health and youth.'"

— Ibn Ajiba, Moroccan Sufi Master (circa 1747-1809)

THE VISIBLE ELEPHANT IN THE INVISIBLE ROOM

Start with death

A tunnel in a haystack
A lease on a house made of solid brick

solid cloud

Inaccessible merriment

Herds of white horses running along a shore
next to a black ocean from

horizon to horizon from which all
forms emerge

All houses we'll live in all houses we'll
abandon or be evicted from

unhousing us as

death is the great unhousing
implacable landlord who

greets us on the way out
as new as if we were born

passing through all language barriers
having left all conceptualizations

as if we had never had them

white tunnel against black crystal
through which coiled rainbows play

research finished
speculations confirmed beyond doubt

Farmhouse with fresh baked bread
against cornfields of spun gold

silk tassels in the wind
bright blue sky

Death a voice
that engulfs us

Addressing us by name with a
tenderness we'd never before known

more melodious than sound
across which white horses'

hooves gently in slow motion beat
in extravagant surf

and our answer is always

“I am here my Lord

Labayk Allahumma labayk

I am here!”

1/29

THE GREAT SAGES SAT DOWN

The great sages sat down to
talk about death

You know —
the elephant in every room

The walls perspired as they chatted
a cat scratched and slept

Somewhere thousands of spiders were
hatching and finding their

way to secluded corners

The room they were in became very
still or boisterously animated

They sometimes demonstrated the
utmost liveliness and then with

long faces the deepest silence

A huge cube of darkness around them
burst into light

They sometimes seemed to be in the
car of a fast-moving train

Each had his or her perspective
and tucked away somewhere

his or her own map out of here
the thin thread back from the

Minotaur into fresh air

"Death is a curse"

"Death is a blessing"

"Death is a doorway"

"Death is a dead end"

Dragons slapped their tails
and fish sped away

The earth's curve could be glimpsed
sliding under sunset's deepening gold

and turned into starry black

One of them had a smile so sweet
when he was drawn back into it

from where everyone sat
and disappeared through it into an

eternal dazzle they were all astonished
but not surprised

grateful for the sense that
words could not convey

as the elephant in every room
shifted its weight from one

foot to the other both front and back

and a scent of musk
(or was it musth?)

suffused the air

1/30

IT'S THE BLACK TRAP DOOR

It's the black trap door inside a
birthday cake

No matter how many slices you cut
that trap door is in every one

divvied up but not multiplied

and everyone has a little frosting rose
especially for themselves

Death the one knock you
don't have to answer to answer

Let's do the road show version
and take it on the road

I can see it up in lights
in Las Vegas

The mega-production
in the Roman Colosseum

Its prints are already imbedded
outside Grauman's Chinese Theater

But I want to talk about your
own footsteps and hand prints and

where they are going

There's so little time
and standing still's

not an option

Does it not make us want to
sing together all the

close harmony songs we know?

Doesn't it make us want to
reach out?

1/30

WILL I STILL WANT TO READ THESE POEMS?

Will I still want to read these poems
if I have that chance

when the end comes?
Will they hold up to stark

reality's scrutiny? Or seem
trivial and beside the point?

Sick in Morocco
I woke up and saw our

hundred-and-one-year-old shaykh's benign face
hovering above me

touching my breast bone with his
divine hand and doing a

prayer for me

An hour later I woke up well may he be
blessed eternally

I can feel his touch on my
heartbone still

God's wind
blowing past my face

so sweetly

1/30

WE DON'T EVEN KNOW

We don't even know if we'll
get out of this present moment

alive

You can imagine all the flying toasters
giraffes leaning down and

licking your face with their
black tongues — you want

all the Jewish lore and paradoxical
tales

all the great Christian pageantry
the Buddhist stillness before

gladiola altars

all the assertions that Allah is The
Only One and the One and Only

God

When we lift our heads and look
the doors and walls are there

the windows with their
wisteria and their snow

and the present moment
sizzling in our ears

1/30

ELABORATE SELF-PROPELLED BIRDS

Elaborate self-propelled birds have been
constructed to take us

above the clouds

where we can eat delectable tidbits
and watch noisy entertainments

while smiling ethereal uniformed beings
tend to our every wish

as we look down through small transparent ovals
at tenebrous turbulent oceans

or patchwork cities of outlining lights below
where doomed mortals are

working out their escape routes
into the unlit blacknesses around them

like the galactic billion acres of stars
around us at every turn

even as we churn through skies
to our purchased destinations

expecting to walk down real stairs into
broad daylight elsewhere than

where we were
when we set out packed with our

few favorite things for another
scheduled sojourn among

palm trees or rocky mountains
solid underfoot

sunlit skies
buildings of glass and wood

like crystal palaces built in
an eternal kingdom whose

only impediments are stop signs
flashing demonic red to occasionally

halt our boundless joys

1/31

THE DIVINE GOLDEN PHEASANT

The divine golden pheasant in the spying room
displays its feathers to no one

A black glove on black velvet
floats in the night

Latches on all our doors are silent
witnesses to patience when not in use

A whisper lives in its own world
listened to by the air

I'm not sure if death rides a white
horse or comes in a rickshaw

or on a palanquin heaped with fruits

out of a dark archway under a
viaduct still in use bringing

fresh water from the mountains

The villagers are more afraid of wolves
and the wolves orchestrate the

stars as if they were on strings
to be worn as proof of

immortality's beauty

In truth everything dazzles
and we don't go down any corridor

secret or not
that isn't illuminated from innermost

beacons

There's always something ominous about
ocean surf at night under a full moon

yet the water in all innocence is only
doing God's bidding by wetting the

shore then sliding back to its source
just as we are every moment of our lives

known in full glory as if we were this
planet's sole inhabitant

not surrounded by everyone else's
sovereignty

which one trumpet blast announces to the
court where all the

courtiers wait to witness

our punctual arrival

the tall windows covered over with
black waterfalls for the event

and a million pianos in their own
drawing rooms playing in perfect

synchronization
the harmony of our souls

where we wear
invisibility within invisibility

in the invisible room
floating on the music of

nothingness

2/1

A POEM AS EXQUISITE

A poem as exquisite
as a day in the country with a

picnic lunch
and in the distance seeing

the horizon of the sea
with a golden sun

singing above it

and as exquisite as that
perfect end-of-day feeling

sliding lightly under the
stars as they each

pinprick themselves alight

A poem as exquisite as a
tiny shell found where water

hasn't been for millennia
of some sea-creature coiled

inside its bony protection afloat or
attached to some

long-gone plant
you slip into your

pocket forget and find again
later delighted by it

like the first time you
found it

A poem as exquisite as a
poem made by hand by

that other hand than this one that
writes them out word by

urged word into a
space unoccupied before by any

poem or perfect day or shell
millenniums old found

lying here still not quite
completely discovered yet now

word by word
articulated word by word left

here to be
seen or heard

2/2

THE EXCURSION

The excursion took us up roads we'd
never thought possible from our

standing position behind the
shadow of our usual diffidence

on every occasion
and our usual defenses of that

diffident position

Our guide wore a cape of bird feathers
and spoke when he ever spoke at

all in a high pitched whisper
heard perfectly even from

three or four hundred people back

Some said it was the shimmering
crystals in the air that transmitted his

words to us
others that we were listening to

ourselves

while a third group said it was
both intermingled

We met no one coming the
other way the whole time nor any other

souls going in our direction that weren't
already in our procession

How did we know each other's names so
readily and the steady gaze in

each other's eyes? The charcoal-like
intensity of light? Even as we faced

mostly forward

over the mighty arched bridge
and the scarlet river?

As we entered unfamiliar territory
we felt we'd been here before

the tree shapes against the sky
the huge circular auras

around the stars
and that we couldn't keep from

flowing forward

casting no shadows
as in a continuous snowfall

the movement in space all around us of
wheeling birds

their cries
the curious telepathy among us

holding to the Prophet's vision
before us

his blesséd heartbeats incorporated
into our own

and the forward elevation of our
spirits

2/3

THE PENINSULA

The peninsula to his left and the
harpooner standing in his dugout on his

right confessed true love for each other
to the applause of dolphins and grunts of

walrus

But to show that all is not
ice and snow in this poem

(in spite of writing this at 3 A.M. to the
silent fall of mute xylophone snow-blobs

in one of 2014s big and
delirious snowstorms)

the palm tree with its dusty spathes
unsubtly indicated its love for the

oasis by moving a few feet closer to it
to the midnight yowls of jackal and

occasional yodels of distinguished exotic birds

Basically love is in the air
as well as in all the other trillion or so

elements this cosmos boasts

and is the passionate amorous crazy glue
that keeps it all together and moving

elliptical and smooth

that if you saw us in true perspective from
outer space not as just another

supersonic chunk of stuff
we'd be a kind of sultry valentine

revolving in place
our moon trying to remember the

steamiest love poems and getting all
pale and pockmarked in the attempt

and our sun as always splitting a
gut in love's pursuit keeping

all her orbits happy as they
dance around her

God-blessed and eternally aloft
in divine gravity's tight embrace

2/4

TO PUTREFY OR NOT TO PUTREFY

To putrefy or not to putrefy
that is the question

To stay in a state of sanctity and
sweeten the grave and the

memories of us all who should happen to stand by it
down the corridors of eternity

as fresh to everyone's nostrils as a
new Spring afternoon or dawn in the

tropics rather than the tragic dark and
rank jaggedness of utter dissolution forgotten

in the long slow tornado of the
future after we've gone

having sweetened each moment among us
as well and furthered

the coiling incense of a generous heart rather than the
shut-down iron tool shack of

rock and ruin that is so many lives
among this planet's rocks

and ruins

intact in this world to His
Glorious eye rather than

spun out of control now and at the
last leaving a trail of wreckage

rather than — *yes why not!* —
of roses happily strewn and

deliciously aromatic like the Prophet's rose-scented
hair in the glass case in Konya

you lean to the corners of to inhale just once
forever and ever —

forever

2/4

IN THE PRESSURE

In the pressure of the ocean
we are all oceanic

But when the ocean recedes
we're left with rules and regulations

sticking up out of the sand

through which we might find some of that
first rapturous crash and sizzle

aligning our poor mud puddle
with that ocean's clear magnificence

that particular way it held itself
and displayed God's Presence

elegantly heaving and majestically
sliding under the stars

2/5

SMALL ENIGMATIC POEM

I went to put away a
plastic container and

two lids from the dish drainer
but when I took away one lid the

other disappeared in a sudden burst
until I realized the second one was

just a shadow cast by the first

2/8

THE ENIGMA OF IT ALL

The enigma of it all stood up and
spread out its feathery arms

All the doubts and gnarly creatures
disappeared from around it

fleeing into scarlet woods and
back into weeping trees

The resplendent enigma straddling the
two worlds and all the others

intersecting them in the tiniest
details of our lives

the true enigma in puzzling feathers

the one of heavy tread and light
repartee

who holds conversations in our heads
yet contains the golden knot of

perfect explanation in its core

as it unravels at the edges into
interesting tassels and addenda

It stands perfectly still
yet seems to do a little dance

similar to the constellations that are
speeding away from us at

supersonic speeds

If it were any more silent it would
burst into everyone's and everything's

voices with their multifarious inflections

which it does in actual fact while
maintaining absolute silence

The famous silence of God that
unnerves the philosophical

but is the rising sizzle of light from
earth upwards

through all of us
at once

2/9

BOWL OF MILK

for Abdal 'Adheem Sanders

We've taken the Middle Path of our
Prophet peace be upon him the way the

man in the assembly filled a large
bowl with milk from a jug and

placed it on his head then took his
hands away rising abruptly but smoothly

the bowl evenly balanced and we could
see the surface of the milk all around the

bowl's circumference glistening but
only slightly shivering

He danced a slow dance to a slow
tambour that hit its dry

beats as his perfectly straight back
brought that bowl in front of

all of us in the huge circle where we sat
gradually accelerating his

pace so you'd think a drop of milk should be
flung out or the whole bowl

topple from his head

Then he began bobbing and
weaving as the beats grew faster

until he was almost whirling with that
bowl of white like a container of

moonlight more than milk catching the
lantern lights and candle

sconces on the flickering walls
with somehow his movements

flickering in perfect time or even
in between beats arms gracefully

scissoring the air the light and
shifting shadows

Now he's moving far too fast to allow
no drop to spill dancing

in strong diagonals his bare
feet firmly placed in small and then

long steps between gliding effortlessly
hands gesturing in the air

The dance lasting a half
hour or more it seems and at the

end decelerating until the drum taps come
evenly but infrequently

and he brings the bowl back to its
place of origin and comes

gradually to a stop
finally lifting his hands for the first time

to the bowl again
and easily shifting it off his head

slowly pouring the entire contents
back into their original container

clearly marked to show that not a single
drop of that precious moonlit milk was spilt

and he sat down again among us
as calm as when he began

2/10

WHEN YOU STEP OUT

When you step out on the wire you're not
sure you'll touch dry

land again or that you'll even
want to so light and buoyant is that

walk in midair with just enough
drag down to keep you afloat

Even the two sides have disappeared
where you began and where you'll

end
and although it looks like death

stalking every step it's rather life that
shivers through your limbs and each

tiny movement neck and brow and
eyes and tingling fingers and toes

You're cousin now to aphids and things that
barely cling to the things of the earth

not flying creatures at home in space with wings
but mortal creatures escaped from their

downward ever narrower and more
harrowing mortality completely

Having left the beginning each step along the
forward line is a meeting-point of

you and God in His most delicate actions
keeping you upright tick by tick

each movement on the wire outlined in
everything you've ever done or seen or

thought though no thought follows you here

It's all shadows in space forests and those
gleams of golden light between shadows

flashes with each flourish shaken silver
residence of non-terrestrial beings and

laughing creatures lighter than the
air itself and balancing horses in full gallop

and the elements released in
marvelous new combinations

You've shrugged off all human notions
you're not going to ever come down and even

headlong to your netless death is a kind of
liberation step after step with each

space in between somewhere like a
million years or more antimatter made

serenely palpable

and when you see the Face of God through
your own eyes up here all

lights and depths and only actual
ascension eluding you

you step out from your body while yet
caring for it with the deepest love

with weight and counterweight and
forward directional most

merciful incorporeal compassion holding your
heavy iron bar that keeps you in

contact with the wire each
step of the way

the bar of heartbeats of your first
actual birth now

closer than ever before to the first and
last breath of God

2/12

THE STRANGE PINK AND BLUE LIGHT

The strange pink and blue light of these
storm-heavy skies

burgeoning with snowy onslaught

Anything could come out of them
A ship of ice with skeleton crew

land right on the house
the rigging electric sparks end to end

The captain cavernous-voiced embodying
all the great tyrant captains in one

Ahabesque Flying Dutchman solid ice figure
glowering at us through the falling flakes

A slowly increasing state of stasis
as snow fills the frames of everything

one by one and all at once
with its evening frozen blanket

chunks blobs wands and
otherworldly castles of Allah's

Beauty and Power

2/13

SUBLIME ARCHITECTURE OF NOTHINGNESS

A perfect snowflake
that has a few million glassy crystals

in cunning combinations never
seen before nor assembled before ever since

the beginning of creation now
falling among its gazillion brothers and

sisters equally unique to the last
angular wedge of ice-rod perfectly

fit against others in geometric utterly
deliriously first-of-a-kind differentness

world within world as it floats softly
gravitationally earthward turning from its

center with spikes spokes intersections shapes and
interlocked knit bits and perfect pieces

sealing in forever a face unseen a
frozen jail whose icy bars jail nothing in but

light the light of trillionth differentiation
from everything and anything that

has come before

a castle a high castle on an ice
mountain so silvery and

high among its crown of bright clouds
uninhabited except by the Uninhabitable

Manufacturer unseen and invisibly hammering
out these spinning parquets for the floor of

earth as a gift from the ceiling of heaven
Who puts into each one the

blindingly and inconceivably delicious
mathematical creativity only something so

beyond human conception could
beyond even the Inconceivable Whose

artfulness knows no galactic bounds as
each flake so designed drifts unencumbered

by a history of design even so distinct is
each one and so unbirthed from its

past so uniquely a universe within
itself as it falls from

perfect anonymity and when it
lands at last and melts away

vanishes completely into anonymity
again

world within world
sinking back into

light within light

and is gone

2/13

PAPAGAGO

Having woken up in Papagago
I wonder if you'd pass me one of those

pineapples over there

Having woken up on Aldebaran I wonder if you'd
take me to to your leader Og

Having woken up in Lower Mongolia
I wonder if I could go back to sleep and

wake up again in *Zee Tristes Tropiques*
where you could let me smell one of those

exploding hibiscus that turn into fireworks

Having woken up in Zongorona Italy
would you toss me a hot ravioli?

Now all's good rather than ten feet of
snow and zero degrees

Now I can wake up in Philadelphia
outside a winter scene so unshaken

one shake of the glass ball we're in might
dislodge it all and

wake me up again
this time where flamingos meet in

zillion flocks and blot the sky with their
neon pink question marks

stretched out flat

2/14

WHAT TENDRILS!

What tendrils!
That connect us when we wake

back to our lives

Swamp or illumined canopy
whose transparency gives us a

God window?

All around us the room arises
and the world

and the inner life's maps with their
moving lips

But to wake in God's precincts
cradled in that place

that the tendrils be Nile reeds
where Moses floated to safety

or the great chains of light
that keep us fastened to His

total dirigible
moving across earth's

shadowy configurations

Tendrils tied to God
that we may be His vertical

“shoes” for
walking in the world

2/26

THE HOUR OF MY DEATH

I haven't seen what time it is
at the hour of my death

The earth obscures the shadow of itself
and life stands in front of the

door of life beyond which death's
going-on is

by its cunning stratagems here for us to
know us by

There's a clock on the wall of it
the ticks obscured by our sweet or sour

conversations
the numbers by that constant visual

fluttering we take as real things of such
grave importance

or is its face facing eternity?
Numberless handless silent?

I hear a long corridor's gentle echo
past little hungry bird flocks

and loud-speakered reverberating train
departures

and each other
distracting us

My wristwatch I'm looking at right now
bashfully hides my death hour

with all its petty appointments and
arbitrary deadlines

a kind of perpetual party of high-spirited
chitchat and the

clinking of glasses

while a distant waterfall seems to get
closer and its divine cascade crashes more

musically in our ears

2/17

THE INDESCRIBABLE WINGS OF THEM

The indescribable wings of them
beating the indescribable air

multifarious rainbow cross-hatches
saturated with oceanic sound

over every kind of known landscape
unknown to humankind

a kind of burnished sulfurous coppery
color unseen and unseeable in

any light and darker than any darkness
in interior or exterior inspiralization

as visualizable as the back of your hand
in a pitch black night with no moon

in which this angelic radiance flows in
every direction at once as

motionless as a single microscopic dot
but also all pervasively swift

over and through immaterial territories
glimpsed like the space between

hairs on an atomic molecule
blown apart in a shredding magnetic

field taking place no when pinpointable
and every possible where at once

as our heartbeats engulf us in an
all engulfing roar

God's Name for God's sake
expounded and exclaimed

in every indescribable space
at the tip of a needle held up

in a shimmering pinpoint of
amorous nothingness

2/19

AT THE END OF THE ROAD

At the end of the road is a door
to the beginning of the road

Trees lining it are the same but
reversed with their arms now

dripping with crystal moss

At some point along the road before we
get to the end

the end moves back through us to the
beginning and the beginning moves along

through us to the end
so the door it turns out is in fact

who is on it both
coming and going

which is
ourselves

hatless and sporting every fancy hat possible
bodiless and wearing all bodily

varieties possible

faceless yet when we get to the door we
enter it only by face recognition

and at that point it's only God's Face
that is recognized

and at that point it's only the
trees that are

singing

2/20

WHEN WE DIE

When we die do we look back with
microscopic or telescopic lenses

and see even the pavement under our
feet every step of the way the grassy

hills and slopes and dips along our paths

The way we caught the cuffs of our
shirts with our fingers before

putting our arms in our coats

The constant clatter in the clutter of our
minds when we awake from

sleep land's
other sights and sounds

Will we see the expressions on

ours and others' faces each of our
moments in space played back

and each remark thoughtful or
thoughtless that soothed and

warmed or wounded and froze
another's warm or frozen heart?

How elements always are rearranged and
still stay the same

How same things are always
utterly new and

obliquely distinct

leaning over the stern of our private death ship
telescopes trained on the

dark departing shore
or over the bow with our new microscopic vision

seeing the deep new place we're going to
atom by atomized atom

place of our father Adam peace be
upon him in primordial

consciousness stretched from horizon to
horizon in God's first outspread splendor

each spiritual soulful tactility
totally alive and

tearfully resplendent with
His Light?

2/21

THE STRUCTURE OF PARADISE

The structure of Paradise must be without
sharp angles or corners straight

lines or perpendiculars
or anything that casts shadows or

dwells in darkness
and everywhere colors are unmitigatedly

prismatic split spectrally into the
shimmering blissful primaries and

mixed ever so subtly with their
transparent edges ever so deftly

overlapping to make variations of purples and
greens sliding across and transparently

through things that themselves have only
the most rainbow of substances

Effervescence here being the great
mode of being

shaping extraordinary cones and caverns
in mountains transforming at

once into habitable spheres of sonic
echoings

and the air itself laden with voices
softly intertwining

Water its actions its ripply thread tremolos
its pervasive expansiveness

throughout gravityless spaces
its throaty gurgle behind every

apprehendable sound
in the valleys caverns and

open spaces no earth nor sky
but only its marvelous

itselfness in constant metamorphosis
and untranslatable essentialness

2/24

DEATH TRIES TO SCRUNCH DOWN

Death tries to scrunch down in
all the major conflicts

but it keeps getting hit
and comes to life

There's that skeleton atop a giant
skeleton horse sailing over the action

blind in both eyes
scythe swinging

Tries to scrunch down to escape
notice between black smudge clouds

Mice in their burrows double up
and the tumult in heaven becomes

stupendously angular
lightning bolts of flashes

carving details out of darkness into
full relief

the most live thing anywhere in life's
slow-motion dance

hooves clattering on no earth nor across
hard tiles

but only on the combustability of air
it tries to scrunch down inside of

harboring no affect of any kind
in the crash of it

death the only live thing
against nowhere

2/26

HAVING JUST AWAKENED

Having just awakened from
one void into another

whose lights and voices intermingle
to give a semblance of life

with animate imagery
stretched out against a blank silver sky

left blank in every dimension to take the
images cast on it

tea kettles trees along highways dream
steam with legs leaping through its

misty puffs

from there to here and back again
mountains Everest-high and lunar-crater low

the inconceivable gamut

while these heart's eyes desire
deliriously delicious landscapes of

escape into tenderer landing places
administered by far tenderer administrators

somewhere between an endless ivory shore
and turquoise lakes in steps

in an air of anatomical embrace
no corner of our souls left out

and the leaping antlered stag of light
set free

2/26

DEATH'S A TINY ALMOST INVISIBLE FIGURE

Death's a tiny almost invisible figure
but when it stands up

it casts a giant shadow that
looms across the wall it makes

between you and the sun

and the swimming planets in their
purple and sulfur zones

and out beyond them
even there its shadow looms

so many bubbles bursting their
planetary debris

I'm seized by a desire to
flip through old photo albums

the kind we don't have anymore
across whose collective face

death's shadows moved out and
down and away

the faces posing there of those
no longer alive

in sepia tints and black and white
already one step apart from their

natural universe of color

between them and the sun
that illuminates all

and the tears of the living fall on the
memories of the dead

who can't feel them
only the speech of the heart

that surrounds their resting place

and the black ocean of Light
we are all in

2/28

THE PARTY OF THE FIRST PART

The party of the first part was
hit with a shot of rainbows

sang high C
and never came down

The party of the second part
watched a sunset whose gold flowed

liquid and opened great
doors onto the full choirs of heaven

— people told him to wipe that
smile off his face ever after

to no avail —

The party of the third part
saw rather than the world rush away from him

cascades of gentle incandescence
pour toward him from its essences

and he swam in its warm bath
to the end of his days

The party of the fourth part

was last seen running with deer
through a snowy woods

as fleet as they and holding his
head held high

The party of the fifth part
heard the thunderous voices of space

and grew suddenly fearless in love
and never looked back

each day expanding its compass
wider

until nothing was left out of its
illumined circumference

And so it goes by Great God's decree
from edge to edge of the

known and unknown universe
and rabbits converse with congressmen

and butterflies sign documents of
human liberation

until every sliver of compassion
of which the earth's portion

in its incomparable vastness is still only a

tiny fraction of the promised
compassion to come beyond this one

enters everyone's beings either at once or
gradually one by one to not

overwhelm us

and the air itself that each creature
breathes becomes a means of

angelic communication between us
as eloquent an

expostulation as any ever heard
and even sweeter by far than any

fervent love song

3/3

AT THE SUBLIME TIPPING POINT

At the sublime tipping point
ladder leaning against

nothingness
each rung a ribbon of light and darkness

gauging itself by the moon's angle
in broad daylight

the inverted bottom teetering
now at the top

worlds rushing by in a
race of apocalyptic wonder

now it's as it always is
but directly evident

Face of God's Mercy pouring through
every adversity

death a single note held in
the billion-note choir

on the tips of our tongues
in our eyes' sudden clarity

in our heart's
supremacy

3/2

THE CLARIFIER

The Clarifier may have other
urgent business and so

can't stay with us long to part
clouds and move heavy

furniture away from the trap
door that opens onto expansive

realization

Moments like flocks of geese above the
house going

north for the winter
squawk in harmonious tones and

pass in the
empty sky

Keeping the mind and heart free from
subject matter

is key to the cavalcade tent's collapse
and the onrush of pure light

of God's good momentary pleasure

which if we breathe in a quick
fragment of is surely

enough for a lifetime of honeybees
making their healing nectar

and passing it up and down the
block to assuage neighbors

for miles around
in our continuously

solitary orbit

3/6

WHEN WE GET UP

When we get up in the morning
we don't know in which direction

the ship will be going

but we should remember we're
on the Titanic and the

song is *"Nearer my God
to Thee"*

that is playing

3/8

THE CREAKING BOARDS OF THE WORLD

The creaking boards of the world are
pulling apart

The hollow hull of the earth creaks from
crest to crest

Night of polar wind
pouring through the

streets and trees
woodcutting the dead ones down

weeding out the dross
thunderously through the air

crashing against pure againstness
with nothing there

but thirty-mile-an-hour winds
cheeks hollow with blowing

everything down
buoyant earth wobbling in the

breach
holding its sides as it

slides in space through
to cosmic laughing

turned to a roaring
river of sheer wind

3/13

IN ALL THE DAYS WE HAVE LEFT

In all the days we have left
could each day be a

thousand years?

Elephant herds move slowly
over the veldt

Bird flocks fill the sky from
tree to tree

Light has no angles but
fits in all angles so easily

we don't notice how it fills in
notches and cracks

never complaining
and though it has its origin

it represents itself as itself
in ubiquitous flow

ever-present in its thusness

But so does darkness

Wild beasts snooze in it

Entangled jungles thrive and
breathe

Nocturnal creatures with
huge eyes find their way

Ants never stop their
industrial business

Could each of our allotted hours
be a lifetime?

Allah leaning forward
to bring us through?

3/14

FOR CERTAIN

For certain
the velocity of a hummingbird and the

velocity of an earthworm are
not the same yet I'm certain

both are satisfied with their progress

For certain
the Sahara under full moonlight

and New York City under full moonlight
are not the same

yet shadows are cast from their
respective objects however they may

obtrude
dunes taxis palm trees skyscrapers

dumb casters of shadows against their
respective floors

I'm certain
the heart of the believer and the

heart of the disbeliever have the

same molecular makeup shape function and

pump their blood as rhythmically

but as Allah says glorified be He He
resides in the heart of the believer

I'm certain serious lightning sonorities
affects compassions thoughts and seismic

movements such as oceans make
cannot be quantifiably nor qualitatively

the same

but might instead be as if both live on
different planetary terrains imbibing

different airs different atmospheres
though God's Grace befall them both

equally and each have equal
opportunity to open their deepest

eyes on His most obvious
demonstrations

3/16

I KNOCK ON THE DOOR

I knock on the door and its
echo fills the night

Night creatures in a neon glow
back into their dark

One star turns in its humming circuit
one cloud crosses it

Silverware tinkles in a distance
of dry twigs crackling

Surf froths up on the earth
or just a sizzle in my ears

No cricket cricks the night with its
crickety creaking

yet everything is singing

Nothing moves anywhere yet everything's
moving

A train horn sounds a steam ribbon
far away that's God's call

nudging me out of the dark
into His Light

3/19

THE SOUND AFTER THE BIG BANG

Was the sound after the Big Bang an
intake of breath?

After *"Be — and it is!"* in all its brilliant
panoply

all its signed particles radiating with their
singing choirs packed deep inside

that still reside through our
shivering beings

fanning in the bright shout in every
niche of space

visible only to the One Beholder Who
within it blows the one breath out

continuously

and the air-sound of highest
silence like horses

gallops still?

3/21

AN ELDERLY BEATITUDE

An elderly beatitude wrapped in
coils of coarse brown wool at the

top cone of a mountaintop
pulled clean air into his lungs before

sailing off to the saints' annual
meeting as the world worked around on its

orbit of night and day
though the one sun in the

distance posits continual day in this
endless universe of continual night

salted with starlight

They gathered on the
head of a pin like a collection of

zeros calculated from a
mortality of prime numbers

whose total amounted to a magnificent
less than zero

that allows God's higher mathematics

to work through its
acrobatical transformations

sweet song on their lips and
astronomical light in their eyes

their outlines constantly dissolving and
reemerging from the perfumed atmosphere

as crucial decisions made not by
them were enunciated and passed from

higher law to higher law to the highest
Throne of all of Allah

from which they originated in the
first place and made into

immortal law at the waterfall's fall of water
and air's radial invisibility

through it all

and the best of them looked in the
eyes of the best of them

down their corridors of purest
emptiness and had only the constant of

God's Name on their lips as the

cogs and gears of the orbiting
planets grind their chains in the

machinery of our ever-existing
God-given being

this world and the next without
end *amen*

3/23

WHAT COULD BE SAID

What could be said that has
never been said?

I come back with a message
from the Land of the Dead?

I'm sitting with saints in a room
knee to knee

drinking a drink that can
make the dead see

We ache for descriptions of
things we don't know

Radiant blessings as fine as
fresh snow

coming from somewhere so
far and arcane

we see as if peering through
down-dropping rain

to a world original
settled in light

God's acres stretched out
to left and right

in infinite alphabetical chains
outpouring each from atomic terrains

suspended in infinitesimal space
reflecting in multiples God's Single Face

in constant circular motion
in God's molecular ocean

3/24

THE SOUL ENVELOPE

Let the sky ring its most celestial bells
and the day start up its most

industrial motors

I'm going through a door to the
other side

with a needle biopsy in the lower
right lobe of my lungs because

nodules in my module have
multiplied in size right in front of our

x-ray vision eyes

and the body is a shiver on the screen of the
lid that keeps our living souls

dry in the restless ocean of the
world

Each day we wear out a little more
on our breathy and breathless

way to His domain
amen

3/24

UNTIL THE VERY LAST BREATH

When we look at death's door it
looks like nothing at all

Blank and featureless
a serious expression on a featureless

face that could be gazing across
empty desert or a crowded room

at a dark frail flower limp on its
stem or a king propped up on his

ermine pillows surrounded by wives and viziers
or at a wall as blank as itself

in front of unfathomable space
full of indifferent planetary matter

whirling to its own music

a camel sleeping by a tent-flap
waiting to be mounted for a month's trek

a plane smoothly gliding twelve hours homeward

a mortally sick pre-teen boisterously
chatting with ten best-friend schoolmates

a lone spider waiting too long on an
unprofitable web in a dusty under-populated

corner

This side of the door is the
only side of the door we can see

Centuries pass through the moment
and it remains the only

side we can see though before it in its
shady light and unambiguous atmosphere

huge ceremonies take place
and backwards celebrations with the

celebrants holding their breath

Oh ocean behind the door of true pure
silence

Ocean behind death's door in us of true pure silence
by the shore of the living and most alive

daily ocean of silence
none of us alone for an instant

from your thralldom's kingdom

have mercy on the little ones and the
afraid

You are God's door in your
starry radiance

standing with no walls in
emptiness of space

each creature eyeing you with
fond hope and expectation

knowing the annals of your
complicated mythologies and your direct

irrefutable invitations

So many symphonies written to
woo you

so many choirs written to call up your
most sympathetic angels to soften the blow

so many doors for each one of us
erected in the stir and softness of

each one's cosmos with their exact
particulars and names whispered or said out loud

God King of all this
King and Master of our allotted breaths

unmistakable recognition as the
door squeaks open a tiniest crack

and one sharp ray of Your Light pours out
even should we live many decades more

in perfect or in dubious health
our own bodies Your

death door behind which our
organs play their parts to the

best of their energies and according to
Your decree's calculated speed

a lightning flash splatter shock above a
sleeping town

the irritable nose twitch on a
deeply hibernating bear

the first smile not from intestinal gas
on a new baby's face

fairy lights over a meadow

bird flocks gathering in a Spring

birdbath ten or twenty at a
time

time suddenly at the end of its
tether with no length left

Let the blast of Your sweet
Mercy never subside on all of us

one creature at a time
and all of us together

at once

Death's door's
silent smart momentary

ding dong bell

tart dewdrop
on our silent tongues

All's well

3/25

HERE IN THE UNDERGROUND LABORATORY

Here in the underground
laboratory of linguistical verification

under golf grass and jungle turf
a few geological layers down

to the sound of bubbling alembics and
Bunsen burners hissing and flaming

by the multiple caged rabbits (for non-lethal
and only occasional experimentation

more to do with natural intelligence and
lusty amorousness)

with Rembrantian light streaming
slantwise by the one round street-level

window in various patched robes of
faux fur and faux fur-lined squares of coarse wool

and hats of generalized nonchalant floppiness
I watch over these poems

devising their
measures and getting their glimmerings in order

such as they are

with the unexpected explosion or
combinatory radiance loosed from

head-on noun collisions or diamond-like
adjectives somehow perfectly fitting

or an abrupt appearance of antlered
young stags bounding headfirst through

complex setups and long-brewing
imaginary soups of the five elements

simmering in actual starlight
blasting back into the deep

woods from which they originally hurtled
at the point of my standing aside in

awe of what only God has wrought
from my impassioned preparatory labors

and the sunset suddenly changes to
dawn

and the villagers awaken to new
shapes and dancing in the streets

dogs merrily barking and the air filled with
deliriously and endlessly whistling and

wheeling birds

as a bright blue sky envelopes us
all in its preternatural brightness

and whisks us away

3/26

SPLENDID AND MORE SPLENDID STILL

1

Splendid and more splendid still
this life and its ribbons its

cantilevers its lemmings lining up to
leap

and the soft landings and the
hard

standing by what's been dealt and
with easy eyelidded glance neither

staring too hard nor slitting asleep
we see Allah's stillness in every

movement and His movement in every
stillness

shaking each horizon awake
and how close the clouds bend to

kiss each passing silhouette

We're hardly here before we have to
take our leave

getting names of things both soft and
hard as well as subtler things and

less subtle things straight

learning silences and the
breaking of silences

eliding into praise songs in the very act of
complaint or condemnation

knowing their key and register
wordy or wordless liltingly flat or enraptured

as happily humming as any passerby
chicken happily grain-seeking or

worm-hunting on its usual circular route around
the pen

2

Pizzicato delegations take to the
high road

Low-throated frog warblers to the
deeper marshes

And every genus and species fills in

between for the universal chorus out-
Mahlering Mahler's Symphony of a

Thousand in sheer shrill glorification until
rafters tremble where there

are no rafters

and thunders from no heaven boom their
responses from underfoot

under paw under claw and webfoot
and a generalized billion part cantata

opens up sound channels even
sound itself never before knew existed

in glory to our Lord in His Present
Absence and Cosmic Presence

overshadowing all shadows and out-
shining all light

Small birds line up on all the
tree limbs

Gnats circulate in buzzier conglomerations

Every viper vibrates and even earth worms
wriggle a kind of oozy maracas

displaying such love in each choired
note you'd

die to hear it

3/27

AS I CLIMB INTO MY DEATHBED

As I climb into my deathbed
next to broken-down warships

dilapidated tenements and lifers in
solitary smoking yet another cigarette

I turn to the wall where all the
pictures come

and this time no unicorns are
left out of the Ark

sound makes ribbons more
golden than sunsets across a

flat white screen

If I narrow my eyes will the past get
perfectly explained and no

loose ends left hanging?

Will something sweet about a
future I won't witness get

tasted and savored in a kind of
solicitous preview?

I won't stay long in this bed
but float out the back window where the

trees are

and the sound of passing vehicles in the
alleyway are actually pavilions on

wheels pulled by serious warriors in
honor of what can be known by us of the

universe both outside and inside us
as sunbeams ratchet through the

pillars of it and flutter across this
bed I get in now

though not really my deathbed yet it
certainly could be

but only my usual imagination run wild
let loose and confirmed at the same time by the

vision of its actual immanence
awaiting prognosis as to the actual when and

where but not by the test specialists and
oncologists

but by a soft voice in a sprinkle of
dewdrops over our house

a dry crack in the heart of the woods
near deer and turtles in their intrepid striving

a strange shaped slice of light in the
sky that flashes red then golden

as it slides up and out into depths of
space I've only conceived of from

here but upon whose body now of
immaterial bulk I ride far into

past this solitary deathbed among
multiple angelic bells

3/28

A LONG WAY

A long way from here to there
but not in terms of

time and space

A long way from here to there
the way growing in this world and

sprouting in the next is

A giant orchid
blowing in unearthly breezes

Beauty that gobsmacks us
one glance alone suffices

The way one breath follows the
next and on and on and

so on

But the upleap could be
unbridgeable

A planet
between us and it

An orbit
that could be cosmos-size

from one sentiment to the next
or state of wisdom

a world's leap
a step-up that's a

step in and a
step out

planting our feet on a
different earth

elephantine vines
and trumpeting flowers

No intoxicant here can
match it

And the fiery light
around each thing

not three dimensional
but eight or twelve

One facet suffices

casts our lonesome
soul onto

God's shore
in a wink that shows

no here nor there
to be a long way to

no time or space
state of Grace

3/29

EVERY SENSATION IN THIS WORLD

Every sensation in
this world and the next is an

electric charge from Allah's domain

a dazzling and vivified expostulation of His
Names and Attributes

puppetized in miniature but
animated by His Light

as we skim across world's ice world's
stage and world's weariness wearing

our smiles and frowns in life's heat's
reflection that's an

arid canyon deeper than sound with
extraordinary crystal outcroppings under an

intense white sky with eagles of angels
ceaselessly circling overhead

their cries calling out
those very same Divine Names

as their eagle eyes that are God's Eyes
scan us below

Multiplicity fans out around us
until we say *la ilaha il Allah*

in perfect pinpointedness and His
resplendent Face appears

as One in its full

dazzling plenitude

and the abyss below us drops
far away from us

to fly free in God's close heart
which is

our mortal heart

freed

4/1

I'M GOING TO LIVE FOREVER

I'm going to live forever

The red rooster on the fence knows nothing
of eternity

The sloops at harbor are already sinking
and even the harbor posts are

breaking into twigs

God take me by the hand
not under these skies with their

variable weathers black holes and
flying machines

The gold door only swings one way
to usher us in

No hoof prints precede us
no globe too heavy to

carry above our heads

What is Your song that You sang in
pre- and post-eternity

that rings us into being?

Would You dissolve it
just as its melody rises?

All poisons are neutralized by our
freedom from mortality

In Your creation elegance takes precedence
over everything

Flocks of circling birds punctuate the purity
their cries like clouds

emitting light everywhere in holy splatters
on the dull ground

4/3

IT'S AN AROMATIC AIR

It's an aromatic air with a
blue stream meandering through it

"Mr. Lundgrin it's your stop sir
time to disembark"

He sees the sitting polar bears the
giraffes and people dancing the

glistening leaves and hears the
plash of water

"Mr. Lundgrin it's Paradise sir and
you're slated to stop here and

take a long deserved rest"

He squints and sees open fields under
sunlight and great draperies of

clouds that surround kiosks from whose
folds music emerges and delicately

intermingles

"Take me farther in" Lundgrin finally
utters in a calm and solemn tone

"But sir this is the destination we
have for you and we must obey

protocol"

Lundgrin's eyes become doves opening their
white wings his face a split

geode with crystals inside his whole
body a lodestone of pure light

So the conductor finally relents and
the conveyance continues

past every gorgeous manifest landscape
impossible to imagine

until there's an open plain both
vast and intimate both outermost and

innermost and stretching out exactly from
where Mr. Lundgrin stops and

everything else begins
and he steps out into it

and takes one step into it
and his heartbeats can be heard

orchestrating angel song as he merges
into it and his own

outline diamond glistens and loses
boundary and gains

sweetness emptiness fullness and Allah's
endlessness all at once

forever

4/3

ALL THE PICTURE BOOKS

All the picture books with their
marvelous pictures

stacked to the stars

crystal boats on mirror lakes so black
the moon the constellations planetary orbs and

cities of the unseen can be
seen in them more clearly than our

own hands in front of us

Giant giraffe-like creatures green and gliding
around us more silent than

eternity is from life's temporal side

One of every people with their beautiful
eyes and moistly enunciated

languages in concentric
circles around us murmuring softly

A vision of space that
goes to all endless depths and

out-of-the-way places
down canals and through

giant underground
geode-like caverns

The best work of our hands and all the
sweetest thoughts of the heart made explicitly

manifest bringing by their manifestation
everyone closer together

A giant diamond bicycle to ride freely
in the free air

a channel directly to Allah's
precincts and directly from His

Presence to where we are
which is always in fact with us

often unbeknownst to us

And peace like a chain of
tropical islands linked by silvery

turquoise blue waters
descending from His Throne

onto our hearts and indelibly
tattooed in them forever

4/4

OUR CAT

Our cat uncanny in her
creaturely ways

crouches patiently

4/4

IF YOU COULD GO ANYWHERE

If you could go anywhere
would it not be where your heart

feels at home among its most deeply
native atmospheres

be it say some tropical place
conch shells on the beach and whitecaps

easily heading shoreward then out
into measureless seas

or somewhere where the plumb diamond of its
natural value and gleam shines most

ardently
and that once that's achieved no

landscape is more dear or more
foreign to it in any universe

once peace has grown all its
glittering vegetation over your heart's terrain

and all levels of swimming are done in warm
clear waters hospitable for every form of

life however slow or swift it might
perambulate

in whatever deeps or
shallows it might

locate?

4/5

OK YOU TAKE THE RIGHT LEG

"OK you take the right leg and
I'll take the left"

"No that would be too easy"

"OK then the face
pull it along easily through here"

"Stop! there's really nothing much to
hold onto

a nose eye-holes chin"

"All right I'll get under the back and
you push him over and we'll

throw him this way"

"No no! Too hard to fling his whole
body from there"

The dialog continues as I sleep and
get up

of just how they'll
fling me among the stars

when I begin reciting the
morning litany

and though I may not quite
feel it that way

certainly terrestrial weight has
fallen away

and a floating turtle free of its
lethargy

is no anomaly

4/7

THERE'S A POD WE CALL THE BODY

There's a pod we call the body
and a landscape we call the soul

While on earth body and soul are
intertwined

Where the body goes the soul goes
but where the soul goes

the body might be left behind

in a dream or a visionary wind
traveling wide awake or

worldly blind

The pod of the body contains what we
need to be alive

The landscape of the soul is a Glory that
stays alive as the pod grows dim

or deathly thin
and the soul grows evermore inward

and the outward grows evermore

earthward
and we face the genderless

Magnificence that is Him

4/7

WHERE GOD GOES

Where God goes you shall go
Where you go God shall go

These words came in a pre-sleep
dialog and distant

zebras pranced in joy their
zigzags making moiré patterns against the

reeds

Nothing can stop you now
all the barriers are down

waves high as housetops may crest and bring
roofs to their knees and

knees to knock at God's invisible door that's
right before us

twenty-four hours of each day of our daily
allotment

Don't book the next freighter or
fighter plane for you really can't

depend on your hopes to extend into any

future plans

Each cloud that passes above us casts its
unique shadow and leaves no

stone unturned

The famous story of the
king who thought to elude death by

building himself inside a stone dome
and as he was putting the final stone in place

turned to find the Angel of Death inside it as well
just waiting for the sense of completion to be

complete

the last stone
sealing him in

Nothing is as remarkable to us as the
possibilities attached to our demise

We hope for certain painlessness and ease
rather than shark teeth or

crocodile bite
and that if we can just avoid sharks and

crocodiles we may
live forever

But the shade pulled down in the
sunny room knows better

and the zebra-induced moiré patterns
resolve into a giant zero through which we

go with a thirst for adventure the way a
speleologist enters a new cave with

headlamp glittering on the hieroglyphic walls

What is it about these lengthy
contemplations

my own *"stay against confusion?"*

Or transfusion transformation into a new
formation on reality's other side

in whatever form God designs and
deigns for us?

Where God goes we shall go
Where we go God shall go

4/11

SAD ALABASTERS PROTRUDE

Sad alabasters protrude from the
sides of happy goblins

Tattered scatterings hang sideways over
once glorious cities' silhouettes

Gold rusts in sudden vaults
and silver tarnishes all who

touch it

Whales wail instead of their usual
deep sea soliloquies across miles

whale to whale

Continents shrink deep into themselves like
shy schoolgirls

Gulls wheel as they spell out a Morse Code of
stuttering sunlight

Steam grates fill with grinning derelicts who
try to get comfortable

Ascetic scholars pull thick wool coats
around frail bodies and

thick dusty tomes full of
calligraphies of sand

I long for a breakthrough into some form of
glorious stammering

but each night can't be a victorious
schooner back from its global voyage

each day can't wait patiently for us at the
bright corner to go for a stroll in

shiny new shoes

I want a sky full of angels pulled taut
across like the sides of a tent

with God's Light shining through
rosily illumining the tent flaps

and an ultrasound of wings
and a sky full of oceanic waves

and a sunlight that hums to itself
in twelve-part harmony

in everyone's hearts

4/12

THE INTRACOIL

Death then life

then death then

life

4/14

WE'RE ON A TRAIN GOING FAST FORWARD

We're on a train going fast forward

landscapes happily passing past us

one thing after another speeding by

spindly wintry trees *en marche* explicitly

one wide smudged window watching them go

And we're rocked gently side to side as we go

A conductor's gruff voice on the PA
startles us

Chitchatting passengers chitchat around us

We stop at a station and idly stand in the
aisles

We slide away from the over-populous cities

Except for a child the car gets silent

We're now so silent we're in another world

4/14

SOME GEOMETRIES

The shore never gets too far away from the
surf

and the sky not too far away from
Matterhorn's peak

Our hearts with their syncopations don't get
too far away from our souls

and on top of it all our heads though
blank as sand or an icy wind

don't get that far away from our bodies
in whatever stretched or

relaxed state they happen to be in

so as adherence is so sweetly the norm
O God don't get too far away from me

don't abandon me to my apprehensions
or lose me down a back alley of any

quizzling thoughts on the
first day of my chemotherapy

where red hot flamingos

stand on one leg even asleep

tortoises climb onto each other
in awkward expressions of love

and sky to peak heart to head and
waves laughingly lapping shores all

over this merry globe carry on Your work
set as testing and strengthening

tasks before us

O be closer to me than I am to myself Lord

Speak to my jugular God of Merciful Mercy

each length of mine away from You a sigh of
longing and each breath closer to You however

many or few
the joy of return

4/15

THERE'S AUDEN'S AND BRUEGEL'S ICARUS

There's Auden's and Bruegel's Icarus
falling from the sky

to no one's particular notice

a barely audible splashdown while a plowman plows
and a shepherd continues herding his sheep

going on about their day bright and
gray-skied as usual

so that our dramatic turns that in no way are
diminished in our eyes and that

use our own mortal bodies for their
dartboards

take place while a dressmaker in the shop
opposite cuts and pins as usual

and the broker on the tenth floor buys and
sells to most everyone's advantage

and some folk are dragged off to a Mozartian

Hell by demons popping up through the

Opera House floorboards while
others are taken lightly by the hand invisibly by

angelic guides who lead through their
secret door to terraced extraterrestrial gardens

yet each blip and tremor however
shallow or deep in us is recorded and

by some strange way not entirely understood
decreed beforehand even in a kind of

déjà vu way that eternally intrigues most
theological savants

and my pain or disastrous medical pronouncement
earth-shattering and sky-opening in my

own particular cosmos

doesn't perhaps affect the gardener happily
clipping hedges and

tending roses

nor the horseman who gallops past

in pursuit of Abraham Lincoln's

soon-to-be-famous assassin
while a bootblack whistles the

same tune he whistles day after day
and a soon-to-be-married bride

turns sideways in a full length mirror
to check her brand new wedding dress

to be worn on the most
important day of her life

4/15

HIS WORDS AS HE SPOKE THEM

None of us here can recount his
words exactly as he spoke them

None of us here can quite remember what he
looked like down (or up) to his eyebrows

one whiter than the other

but of the space his constant prayer inhabited
and the walk he took through this world always

focused on the next
there are many who can't quite describe it

but whose own lives were transformed by it

Tree boughs can feel a difference in the
fuzz of their ends

birds loop through a transmogrified air in their
flights

doors open in space that before were
sealed tight

and all by the space that opened out
around him with each breath of his

making their own celestial engineering in the
way things move or seem to move both

before and within us very distinctly
other than the way things were before we

saw him or sat with him in his
night silence like a black hole that hums to itself

as it siphons all matter
into its maw and presents a

placid face to us with our
own various facial expressions of awe that become

absorbed by the singularity of his
own in

infinite multiplications

4/15

ACACIA TREE POLLEN

Acacia tree pollen blows yellow through the
1940s Oakland California air

fine and rich
and I was allergic to it after multiple hospital tests

and had to go every week to get an immunization
shot from a scary nurse who took a

fresh vial of serum out of a giant fridge and
sucked it into a seemingly equally giant syringe

that she then poked into my seven year old
arm I noticed

even then was frail and spindly compared to that
evil needle that cured me of my allergy

until decades later in the 70s when we lived for

some weeks maybe months in Murcia Spain
birthplace of Shaykh al-Akbar Ibn al'Arabi

and the town was awash in those powdery yellowy
acacia trees and I could feel my

lungs closing up a bit making it
harder to breathe in the holy birthplace of that

great and enigmatic saint also a Leo
like me Herman Melville Shelley and Arnold

Schwarzenegger but I'll stay with all but

Arnold Schwarzenegger in terms of vision and
linguistic accuracy

as the fine yellow powder I had my first
earthly intimate relationship with

blows through 21st century air
my little lungs now reluctantly hosting a few

interloper cancer cells that may Allah
please take back to Himself

before He takes
me

4/16

WHEN DEATH TAKES OFF ITS MASK

When death takes off its mask
there's only one face behind it

When death takes off its shoes
the stairs become evident

When death sits down to have a smoke
we're eager to arrive

When the ship pulls away from earth
we're on it

When earth pulls away from us
we're not on it

How many have gone before
and we didn't notice?

By a strange mathematics
it's always someone else

The air is filled with light
and our time has come

Even if we live more years

steam puts its

mist on our windows

We're still here and will
always be here

through it all
ever more beautiful

and still

4/18

ORPHEUS WORE THAT LOOK

Orpheus wore that look of astonishment for the
rest of his life

How could he have been so
thoughtless as to turn around?

And so near the top?

Wasn't hearing her behind him on the
steep gravel enough?

It was all dark anyway and he couldn't
have made out those features that

so swung him around

In the end Majnun even says he doesn't want to
actually *be* with Laila

He has Laila inside him

If we're given a command and its
conditions knowing full well breaking it

entails disaster

what crazy mechanism inside us
whispers its shaytanic hiss to

flagrant disobedience?

Adam and Eve! Back to the original
in the leafiest loveliness known

plucking fruits at our pleasure
and being held accountable for our

wrong move so deeply inspired
a split second of

colossal miscalculation we
pay for for the rest of our lives

The two beloveds almost floating up the
steep incline from the Underworld

They could feel the upper air's fresh
breezes on their eyelids and cheeks

Orpheus could have evermore sung his joy

Is this an explanation for the
rough time we have here?

We can't control ourselves to do what's
right?

Is lament the real song we sing
each time we sing?

Even as we dress it up as *"Orpheus:
The Musical"*?

Do we own any of this?
Is our own phantom lurking around in the

shadows to curse us?

Can't our clear face face God and
win the day?

Can't the Prophet's mere gorgeousness in every
act of his control us?

God's Peace seal us in His embrace?

4/19

A DOVE'S COOS

A dove's coos the first sound I
hear out the window

Then hissing of waves
but that's in my ears

God's delicate Voice along spring branches
coaxing the leaves to push out to fan-size

to catch the sunlight

Then my wife closing a door or
opening it

Cars on the street farther away momentarily
swooshing

Air and inside it space's more
mysterious corridors

But the dove coo keeps falling and
falling like a sweet feathery

hammer falling on an old leftover snowflake
that at the fragile

coo-stroke turns turquoise

4/21

HERE'S THE WINDOW

Here's the window you
can't climb out of

Here's the banquet you
cannot eat

Here's the sunlight that
showers another world

Here's the life you can't
repeat

Tigers each side of the
road you travel

hungrier than time
to swiftly devour you

You can't avoid them so
don't even try

Those who survive them
are very few

The key is held in the
hand of a saint

One turn in the lock is
all it takes

But how to turn it you
must be taught

somewhere between hope and
deep heartbreaks

The less you become the
greater you are

Shaving down is no
easy task

Have heart without ceasing
alone in the universe

The answer comes each
time you ask

The door won't open so
don't bother knocking

Your soul dwells already on
the other side

Go through yourself as

through a door

and in God's Light and
Grace abide

4/21

EACH DROP OF WATER

Each drop of water is a
future glimpse

when we evaporate
into God's greater atmosphere

We drink His Plenitude
as our inner dry rocks

glisten with His Light

The drop contains the ocean
as the ocean dissolves the drop

We drink an ocean with
each drop we drink

and we evaporate

Were we ever anything more than
future evaporation?

Each of our actions drop by drop
filling our ocean right or wrong

from shore to shore of our

possible span

whose continents lie under it
ready to emerge

when we're gone

echoes of gulls in the air
left behind

God's surf on the sand

crawling its elegant foam
as we return home

4/23

APPROPRIATE APLOMB

I'm going to go down a long hall
and sit in a leather reclining chair

under an overcoat of prehistoric earth

Elbows and femurs might stick
out a bit at the sides

but a strong Sahara sunlight at a
sharp and acid angle will play on the

equally angular planes of my face

as a drip of venomous healing serum
pulses through my main arteries

hunting down the squamous cancer cells that
fled my tongue and now

colonize my lower right lung

It's early yet and the
cat still thinks I smell OK

So though sharks somewhere in shark dark
deeps are following a trail of blood to its

deliciously vulnerable source

and planets somewhere are either
dehydrating or melting their permafrost into

habitable lakes under tectonic plates
light years away

a very distinct God-Light shimmers in the hallway
and in the deeper folds of the chair where I

sit submitted to the gauntlet God's thrown down
with I hope

appropriate aplomb

4/25

LORD YOU FOUND ME

Lord You found me where I was
and in the condition I was in

and blessed me

out in the open air or in deep
dark seclusion

from inside me way inside the deepest deep
inside me or of my dissolving

body as it shakes my soul free

and no escape no
getting up from Your tight grasp and

walking away saying *"OK I'm
done"*

until You Lord are well
done with me

Cancer and the miseries of its harsh
treatment our tsunami

with boats left
up in trees and the

village poisoned flat the
villagers not praying five times a

day now but ten or twenty
to get it right Lord

in Your tender care and tenderest
Mercy

4/26

IN A TRIAL BY FIRE

In a trial by fire you might
need to step lively

keeping cells and molecules
a step ahead of the flames

or else keeping them at bay with the
godly asbestos of your great

watery light

I imagine Sayyedina Ibrahim in the
pit of fire as cool as a cucumber

flashing prophetic protection as God's
Messenger and icicle of faith

no flame could lick

And if the fire is from the inside out like
chemotherapy

its dry crackles noticed on scalp and around
nostrils and tongue

one step ahead in determined patience

is all it takes
to stride forth unscathed?

Sayyedina Ayyub scratched his
boils with pottery shards

You can hear the scritch-scratch all the way
to now

and his agony none lessened

But as the body boils in flickers the
eyes may be dancing with delight

for no hand is above God's Hand
and nothing outside His command

each flame lick love at its rawest
freshest and most

erotic embrace of all

when fold after fold of Paradise is
rolled into Hell's creases and

cracks

each flame that licks us in

whatever ordeal a

glimpse through the Gate at His
cool sweet promise to come

4/27

INNER CORE

I'm alive
like a ball of string

around its inner core

FLICKERING SHADOW

The kind of shadow a huge
suspension bridge makes on the

fast flowing waters below

The kind flamelets along edges of a
desert fire make against the

gravelly earth alongside them

The kind of shadow a bee makes
honing in on a flower between

it and the sun

This world wakes on the shores of the
next where the shadow itself is

perfectly silent and hardly hints at the
life held within whatever makes it

so also in the next world another
kind of aliveness lives that somehow makes of

this world a flickering shadow giving a
gorgeous semblance but being in

fact a flat black silhouette against a
shore of untold riches topazes amethysts

and silver nuggets as small as
distant stars strewn across

untold miles of space

and here we are with our
pain and suffering itchy scalps and

fear of death

leaning out over reality like a
shadow

unable to count the blessings that have been
scattered and collected upon us

one bee-flight at a time

one nectar sip in broad daylight
and we're gone

5/2

AS A SNOWDROP BIG AS ALL TEXAS

As a snowdrop big as all
Texas might be said to resemble

nothing so much as the great sky itself
gazing down at little earth from its

blue cosmic perspective

and just as a flake of skin might in
no way bring to mind the vast deeps of the

entire world's oceans interlinked and
basically contiguous

and just as you and me in our
mortal dimensions might be said to

barely measure up to the early giants
said to predate all our prehistoric

gentry of all ethnicities and locations

so after all of this world itself
held between thumb and forceful

forefinger of space over a dizzying abyss

so each gulp of ours each vein-twitch of
pulse each thought pulse sweetly

hammering vacancy with just at least an
inkling of this world or the next in both

proportion and ultimate meaning
no god but God

and each lisp of imperfection praising
absolute mathematical and

all theological perfection itself

even if we only approximate it by our
willingness to imagine it in

terms we can at least basically
comprehend

no god but God
chasing away bats and spiderwebs

no god but God
tolling the bells of the most

ancient campaniles
no god but God

raising whales' heads up from the
surface of the seas

in mammalian agreement with its
totality of beauty

no god but God
uttermost agreement and agreeableness

with every truth imaginable and the
very most unutterable truth forevermore

no god but God

amen

5/4

HIS GOOD PLEASURE

Perhaps it's not the universe that's
slowing down or speeding up

or closing its little secret drawers
or drawing its major curtains together

calling all its doves back into the ark
or loosing all its cats big and

small back into the wild

sucking back all its circulating waters
and pulling the plug on all its

backup and buildup to sluice through its
remoter and pickier drains

as we bob here on galactic surfs
keeping our fool heads as much as

possible above water

but it's just ourselves that are like
the windmills our own Quixote natures

tilt against running up time after
time with our sad lances drawn

wondering if they're actually monsters
or simply turning their blades to

grind the daily grain

and whether the flickering lights of
nights and days are cosmic occurrences

or the natural shutters of our
beings louvering on and off

and if we are the universe then
may it shine and darken as its

Master pleases

and may His pleasure somehow always
be our own

5/5

THE TIPS OF MY FINGERS

The tips of my fingers are like
explosions in a salt mine

My body like a ship boarded by
brigands

Some serious eclipse is taking place
and I'm not sure which is the

planet and which the sun
(or is it the moon?)

I know my blood is keeping up with the
chemo infusion

I can hear it inside knocking the
spiders out of its shoes

It's a long drop down to the
shores of Paradise

and our skins are already a bit
snagged on the

sharp edges of its corals
but the beat of its blue waters

invoking Allah's Name with each
stroke is enough to

lure us on

I'm at a murky window looking at all
this happening on the

other side

where it seems more and more to me
there is no other side

but only the evanescence of our
selves

and God's bright skies alone our
astrolabe

5/7

FINALLY

Finally I've gotten what you're doing —

You're celebrating every instant of your life and

expanding it into a cosmos

5/8

POISONED FROM INSIDE

I'm being poisoned from inside
and the anti-poison poisoner is knocking on

all my veiny arterial doors to find the anarchists
hiding as I breathe around them

hoping to diminish them
entirely before I myself am

entirely diminished

And how will it do that?
Somehow penetrate their

soft shells to their fully alive and
obstreperous interiors

and we know so well how tenaciously
life clings to life

so the cancer cells in all their proprietary self
satisfaction

won't go easy

and the poisoner will nutrify itself

in potent strength to counter their strength in this

innermost cellular chess game taking place
on my physical plane

while my soul increases its hold on the
Unseen begging God's Mercy as all this

tumult like a slow twister
takes place inside me

just another passing body on the planet
but my body after all and a

truly viable and valuable vehicle since birth to
carry me to a determined but to

me so far indeterminate forward

O poisoner do God's job on these
interlopers and treat them

with all your stern decisiveness

all in God's will from start to
finish

not one nanosecond left to chance
as we extend our hopes

realistically to the eternity of our

perfect hearts

5/9

IN THE MIDDLE OF

It's hard to know where the
"middle of the night" actually is

or *"the middle of the forest"* or the
"middle of a sentence" or

*"you interrupted me while I was in the
middle of a thought"*

unless we apply exact digital
measurement perhaps and get the

mathematics exactly right

or as Dante says *"in the middle of the
journey of our life"*

when paths with their
wild beasts confront us

right here in our middles or rather our
life's journey's middles

and I'm up now
awakened in the middle of the

night in the middle of nowhere
to visit the bathroom

and wonder if being in a middle might mean
all things stretch out

equally at our sides
so that here in space its extreme

wings might include say the
pyramids of Egypt or Argentina's

pampas grasses stretching for miles to the base of the
sierra mountains

and if we're in *"the middle of space"*
does it pinpoint a spot whose

extensions are the curious
wraparound of time and space that might make a

kind of flying ring in cosmic totality
in which we as

sentient mortals smack in the
"middle of our lives" now

find ourselves?

5/10

IN THE WORLD OF BODIES

In the world of bodies
a polar bear might be

equivalent to the President of Brazil
a koala bear to the planet Mars

There's something the same about all
created things

hard or soft falling or rising evading our
touch or embracing us breast to breast

with starlight shooting through it all from its
stellar perspective

a smile lost in a crowd
a shout on a mountaintop

astronauts reaching for their powdered
breakfasts floating in space

all molecular beings charged with God's
Mercy in a textured manifestation as

far as our eyes and conceptions can
conceive

How sweet it all is!
That God's rain might

fall on it all equally from
Timbouctou to the oceans

blue or black yellow or
rainbow purple on some unseen planetoid

hiding in hyper-galactic swirl

while here below a bit of
moisture on the corners of my lips

a flick of eyelids and a clearing of
throat

as the soft music of silence
slips in through our ears

5/12

NOSEBLEED

As if all one's life were reduced to

stopping a nosebleed

5/12

ENDLESS SINGULARITY

Is a tree that has never tried being a
woodpecker less a tree?

Is a square that never tried being a
circle wheeling down a hill that

never tried being a tall mountain or a
mountaineer walking through its

rocky thighs and armpits
any less a square

doing what a square say as the
basis of a box or cross street

intersection does best and as
none other in all God's

creation can do as well?

Ocean becomes sky and sky falls as
rain on tops of heads as well as

picturesque orchid swards in the
Swat Valley blowing their delicate

purples in the bluest of airs

We strive uphill and down
even when we wake up from the night

our feet just touching ground again
and just as we are should we

try to be what at that moment at least
we're not?

I mean except for sainthood of
one kind or another and supreme

enlightenment that's in God's purview anyway

just how and who should we

strive to be?
Redwood tree or woodpecker beating out its

staccato vibrato elsewhere in the
wood as mist fills the forest with an

atmospheric ambiguity?

O love Who is our Lord in every
transformation from

state to state and molecule to

molecule like trained ponies

agile to Your call

bless us just as we are with yet a
dimension of greaterness always

circulating around our deepest interior
so that we may be

tree and woodpecker circle and
square and all your variations in between

for Your good pleasure of the vast
multiplicity of being facing

Your implacable Unity always
Glorious in its endless singularity

5/19

LONGEVITY

All longevity is
mere brevity

5/20

ENGINES ALL OVER THE WORLD

Engines all over the world
are starting up right on time

Ophelia appears in her black door
singing fragments of medicinal flowers

as the river below her ripples its
invitation

Birds don't have to adjust their flight much
unless they fly between branches

which they do uncannily well

Statesmen both pure and corrupt
raise hands or lower them as their

state stumbles forward over our
bodies politic

A French merry-go-round at the
foot of the grand stairway in Montmartre

merrily goes round with five
schoolchildren in their school

uniforms cursing like drunken sailors

On a mountaintop a romantic poet in a
black coat opens wide his

arms in joy at the sunrise while
mountain goats climb

giddy heights straight up impossible
rocks

A boat churns toward port with the
next emperor aboard who's only

twelve and already has the
stern look under his gold hat

of an eighty-year-old monarch

Ripples in the air unseen mirror
ripples in water and earth ripples

unseen underfoot of seismic
breathing

as we walk our way in trusting
security from one destined point to the

next leaving worlds behind us and entering
worlds before us with unsung

songs on our breaths
and unseen worlds on our

eyelids rivaling the visions of Kubla Khan
in extraordinary detail of golden

filigree and screeching peacocks

each step a flowering in God's Garden
here in the present tense even as it

fleetingly vanishes away

each step a gong on the world's
gamelan each strike of our

glorious heartbeats on the sky's
implacable xylophone of peace beyond

comprehension

5/20

I'VE GOT MY DEATH INSIDE ME

I've got my death inside me

It's in a little jeweled box the
size of the universe

held aloft by two strange angels
one black one white and both

invisible though their pure smiles
reverberate all the fanning and stuttering

colors of the visible spectrum

the jeweled box hollow and resounding with a
clock's precision

Gazing inside it you see flat country full of
ceaselessly leaping gazelles

and every atmospheric condition possible
on this and every other planet in

God's unending creation

There it is!
lodged deep there within —

a friendly notion in my daily rounds

awake when I'm asleep and
asleep when I'm awake

My death deep inside me
like a saint at prayer with his

knees drawn up to his chin
and the walls of his cell

range after angelic range of
shattering light to Allah's Throne

perpendicular to all that is
horizontal

already accommodating me

5/20

ON THE RIM OF THE WORLD

On the rim of the world
dangling our legs

the cosmos revolving around us

how beautiful the light and dark of it
deep black that seems to

go on forever
sparks of light in their

planetary motions like
ringlets of pearl dipped in

liquid gold and
splattered with silver

reflecting so many rambunctious
suns bursting at their

own seams seemingly
infinite and eternally glowing

as one after another there and
farther in even deeper space

shines in uttermost brightness then

in a burst disappears

here as we sit here
in the surprise and constant of

every moment

holding our breath and
letting it go

it all simultaneously taking place
within us

or maybe originating there
how can we know for sure?

dangling our legs here
on the rim of the world

5/21

ALIVE FOR NOW

Alive for now
my face pokes into a cloud

and looks around

Oh the melodies that thread through
the trees

and slide along the ground and
come up through our feet!

Babies dance their measures
sensing the world swirl around them

and each gulp of air in our lungs
an eyelid blinking in this

world onto the next in its most
arboreal splendors

Alive for now
like the breath of a horse

right at our ear
not the stallion of endless night

but the faring forward spirit in
manifest honesty

hair sleek as the wind itself
and glistening with God's

special caress

Alive for now
all we can count on in

this world
surrounded by doors and walls and

lush landscapes
and faces that come up to ours with

good advice

Alive for now
in the next few seconds

and the train whistle across town
heard in these ears

5/22

IF SOMEONE

If someone were to pull the plug and
drain the water of the oceans of their

water

or take a pin and puncture the air of its
air

or tread underfoot the spiritual
basis of all that is

in an agonized
squelch of tight materiality

and we were left on earth
trying to catch our breath and

failing

and even our own bones rebelling
against us

and our hearts crashing inside us

and our eyes unable to focus on
anything but a vapid blur

and this poem occurred and
continues but I'm at a loss as to how to

end it

The entire universe sucked backwards
back to its explosive origin

which would of course end it all including this
poem

bang whimper or whatever so beyond our
wildest comprehension

in a blink of time if at that moment time
could be thought of as blinking

and of course none of us would be
mercifully left to witness it

long gone into the generalized vacuum
Job and his detractors and all else

beside

and only a hush remained

and not even a hush

5/23

THERE'S THE EARTH

There's the earth
shifting and sliding and
pouring itself as usual

There's materiality
evanescing then popping into
hard intransigent form
then melting like candlewax
into amorphousness

There's mortality
extending then decreasing then
counting the days and the
hours with high hopes and
faith in a
pleasant outcome
ending in death and the
soul's immortality

Then there's Allah
above and over all
throughout all the all that
is in all its
entirety
and all else perishing and
unreal and always remaining the
all that is

and that sweet filmy taste that
remains
that high hum of sizzling choirs
that light that casts no
shadow

That extensive endlessness
that wry butter in our mouths
that sometimes becomes
eloquence and sometimes
a stuttering awe before God's
endless flow

Then there's something
then there's nothing

and our hearts strong enough to
bear it

and our intellects not
strong enough to understand it

and our wise eyes that see it
right in

front of us

5/27

DEATH IS STANDING UP FULL HEIGHT

Death is standing up full height in the
next world

dusting ourselves off and the
dust flakes are this world in all its

complicated dimensions and what's left is
what good we've done

glistering like a suit ready for
swimming in the next world's

clear atmospheric waters
filling all space

from end to end of
endlessness

We stand taller there than we
do here

though there it's dimensionless
and the glass bells of our breaths

chime in the glorious trees
and the beats of our true hearts

rustle over precious stones in
symphonic river beds

and the air we pass through is our own
transparent movements there

where there is nothingness
but God's Sumptuous Reality greater than

this one which is dust made beautiful
until you touch it and it

drifts away into oblivion

There spectacular High Definition reigns

into which we enter more fully than we
ever entered here

and donkeys with cloud wings ride us
wherever we want to go

and fanning lights in colors we've never before
seen manifest

everything

6/1

"AND HE SURROUNDS ALL THINGS" (Qur'an)

God calls us as well through our
reluctance as through our replies

The dead heart knows God as great as the
live one

or greater

The gray sky that lies heavily over the
plain has the lightning and sunlight within it

enough to illuminate all rough crags and
crevices

Our resistance to God in any given moment
in the silver tent of God's intimacy

at the base of His blue mountain of
our ascent stumble by stumble

may bring us closer to what God
wants for us than what we

think we want from God
Who is All-Giving any time a moment

falls to us
which is at every breath and every

next breath
after that

Constraint and the caged-in feeling
gives way to a teeming jungle of

wild cries of delight and tropical
birds of light

whose raw colors dazzle the eye
and the faint call at the

end of our visceral corridor is the
only one we'll hear that

calls us by name out of sheer
cacophony

each note of which is purest
silver and softest

gold dug from God's
deepest and darkest mines

6/2

IF ONE TINY THING

If one tiny thing in the universe were
out of place

it would all grind to a halt

and a gulf of silence cover us all
in a drowning wave

Each particle put here by Perfection
each difficult breath or eye blink

Oh God so perfectly in place and fully
operative as You see fit

beyond our capability or comprehension

in the molecular chain through
everything whose faces like bright

children are turned in
adoration toward You and

You Alone

just as we are
no matter where we face

in our obedience and abeyance

here in the shadows of the girders
held in place by Your angels

to protect our heads in their
extravagant thoughtfulness

though a tiny light in everything
shine like a sun

in the darkest pit of Your Mercy
amen

6/5

SEEK OUT THE STARLIGHT

Seek out the starlight in your
searchlight

all corners illumined by your beam

The door perpendicular to
horizontal oceans with their

rough waves

Swing in a tight circumference
sliding past treetops in their

usual sway

Each eyebeam a semaphore for
true sight

Each ear twitch the underbrush
rustle

Our bodies with their cantilevers
set forth into the

sunniest glades

We've all seen the

undertaker at the door

with his unpretty smile
a lone and lonely figure

in a shadow

His face like ours and his
voice a near perfect match

but his vitality negative to our ongoing
positive

and his influence not beyond
his own door's height

We can't pass him by completely

but invite him to our table
before the meal gets cold

If we enter into conversation
his scowl will recede

our light always landing on the
high places

its arc wide taking in everything

We're not here long enough to
catalog our bones

but just long enough for eternity to
invade us forever

starting now

6/16

FLUTTER

It's all a slight flutter in the air
and then we're gone

Flash in the mirror that is God's
mirror in nowhere and in particular

right before us in which we see
in seeing's high domain

Alp-like in its exaltedness and near to
the swiftness of clouds

Valleys of fluffy nothingness wrapped around
entire galaxies in a heartbeat

flake falling outward from its
innermost source

Our faces tell the tale before our lips do
and our bodies in their

service to Allah and His Beloved in every
circumstance in their arch or straight-backed

silhouette with light flashes around their
outline as we move through God-space

to meet God where He is
in the very divine rafters of His hall

Beowulf's mead hall the universe itself
whose vapors intoxicate us into

being and out again into God's
Greatness profusely star-lit

Our true life begun

6/17

THE HIGH TOWER

The high tower that is such a perfect
viewing place for the

less accessible stars

The burnished bronze ladder of light
that connects earth and heaven

The short stool that extends our
stature upward only a few yards

then lower places among crowds in
back streets in barrios

Dense forests where we could run
into a saint but it might be

less likely

Teeming markets where smiles are
as abundant as scowls but at

any moment a brawl could break out

Then canals where sampans transport
bushels of wheat or cloth and

an entire family lives most of its
life below earth level on

a river's variable waters

until finally we are lowered into the
earth itself and our viewing is

done but new eyes open on unimagined
sights each more

stupendous than the last

These viewing places all in the
heart and the most desirable

visions just within capturable reach
even just beyond our

weak eyesight to comprehend

as every vision resides with God in His
All-Seeing domain

though our ticklish feet can find no
solid ground to stand on

and our interiors like cascades of ever-
fresh waters glisten in His

onrushing
ever-present daylight

6/18

INDEX

ABOUT THE AUTHOR

Born in 1940 in Oakland, California, Daniel Abdal-Hayy Moore had his first book of poems, *Dawn Visions*, published by Lawrence Ferlinghetti of City Lights Books, San Francisco, in 1964, and the second in 1972, *Burnt Heart/Ode to the War Dead.* He created and directed *The Floating Lotus Magic Opera Company* in Berkeley, California in the late 60s, and presented two major productions, *The Walls Are Running Blood*, and *Bliss Apocalypse*. He became a Sufi Muslim in 1970, performed the Hajj in 1972, and lived and traveled throughout Morocco, Spain, Algeria and Nigeria, landing in California and publishing *The Desert is the Only Way Out*, and *Chronicles of Akhira* in the early 80s (Zilzal Press). Residing in Philadelphia since 1990, in 1996 he published *The Ramadan Sonnets* (Jusoor/City Lights), and in 2002, *The Blind Beekeeper* (Jusoor/Syracuse University Press). He has been the major editor for a number of works, including The *Burdah* of Shaykh Busiri, translated by Hamza Yusuf, and the poetry of Palestinian poet, Mahmoud Darwish, translated by Munir Akash. He is also widely published on the worldwide web: *The American Muslim, DeenPort,* and his own website and poetry blog, among others: www.danielmoorepoetry.com, www.ecstaticxchange.com. He has been poetry editor for *Seasons Journal, Islamica Magazine*, a 2010 translation by Munir Akash of *State of Siege*, by Mahmoud Darwish (Syracuse University Press), and *The Prayer of the Oppressed,* by Imam Muhammad Nasir al-Dar'i, translated by Hamza Yusuf. In 2011, 2012 and 2014 he was a winner of the Nazim Hikmet Prize for Poetry. In 2013 he won an American Book Award, and in 2013 and 2014 was listed among The 500 Most Influential Muslims for his poetry. The Ecstatic Exchange Series is bringing out the extensive body of his works of poetry (a complete list of published works on page 2).

THE WORKS
(Books of poery published and unpublished)

Dawn Visions (published by City Lights, 1964)
Burnt Heart/Ode to the War Dead (published by City Lights, 1972)
This Body of Black Light Gone Through the Diamond (printed by Fred Stone, Cambridge, Mass, 1965)
On The Streets at Night Alone (1965?)
All Hail the Surgical Lamp (1967)
States of Amazement (1970)

Abdallah Jones and the Disappearing-Dust Caper (published by The Ecstatic Exchange /Crescent Series, 2006)
'Ala ud-Deen and the Magic Lamp (published by The Ecstatic Exchange / Crescent Series, 2011)
The Chronicles of Akhira (1981) (published by Zilzal Press with Typoglyphs by Karl Kempton, 1986; published in Sparrow on the Prophet's Tomb by The Ecstati Exchange, 2009)
Mouloud (1984) (A Zilzal Press chapbook, 1995; published in Sparrow on the Prophet's Tomb by The Ecstatic Exchange, 2009)
The Crown of Creation (1984) (published by The Ecstatic Exchange, 2012)
The Look of the Lion (The Parabolas of Sight) (1984)
The Desert is the Only Way Out (completed 4/21/84) (Zilzal Press chapbook, 1985)
Atomic Dance (1984) (am here books, 1988)
Outlandish Tales (1984)
Awake as Never Before (12/26/84) (Zilzal Press chapbook, 1993)
Glorious Intervals (1/1/85) (Zilzal Press chapbook, ?)
Long Days on Earth/Book I (1/28 – 8/30/85)
Long Days on Earth/Book II (Hayy Ibn Yaqzan)
Long Days on Earth/Book III (1/22/86)
Long Days on Earth/Book IV (1986)

The Ramadan Sonnets (Long Days on Earth/Book V) (5/9 – 6/11/86) (published by Jusoor/City Lights Books, 1996) (republished as Ramadan Sonnets by The Ecstatic Exchange, 2005)
Long Days on Earth/Book VI (6-8/30/86)
Holograms (9/4/86 – 3/26/87)
History of the World (The Epic of Man's Survival) (4/7–6/18/87)
Exploratory Odes (6/25 – 10/18/87)
The Man at the End of the World (11/11 – 12/10/87)
The Perfect Orchestra (3/30 – 7/25/88)(published by The Ecstatic Exchange, 2009)
Fed from Underground Springs (7/30 – 11/23/88)
Ideas of the Heart (11/27/88 – 5/5/89)
New Poems (scattered poems, out of series, from 3/24 – 8/9/89)
Facing Mecca (5/16 – 11/11/89) (published by The Ecstatic Exchange, 2014)
A Maddening Disregard for the Passage of Time (11/17/89 – 5/20/90) (published by The Ecstatic Exchange, 2009)
The Heart Falls in Love with Visions of Perfection (6/15/90 – 6/2/91)
Like When You Wave at a Train and the Train Hoots Back at You (Farid's Book) (6/11 – 7/26/91) (published by The Ecstatic Exchange, 2008)
Orpheus Meets Morpheus (8/1/91– 3/14/92)
The Puzzle (3/21/92 – 8/17/93)(published by The Ecstatic Exchange, 2011)
The Greater Vehicle (10/17/93 – 4/30/94)
A Hundred Little 3-D Pictures (5/14/94 – 9/11/95) (published by The Estatic Exchange, 2013)
The Angel Broadcast (9/29 – 12/17/95)
Mecca/Medina Time-Warp (12/19/95 – 1/6/96) (published as a Zilzal Press chapbook, 1996)(published in Sparrow on the Prophet's Tomb, 2009)
Miracle Songs for the Millennium (1/20 – 10/16/96) (published by The Ecstatic Exchange, 2014)

The Blind Beekeeper (11/15/96 – 5/30/97) (published 2002 by Jusoor/Syracuse University Press)
Chants for the Beauty Feast (6/3 – 10/28/97)(published by The Ecstatic Exchange, 2011
You Open a Door and it's a Starry Night (10/29/97 – 5/23/98) (published by The Ecstatic Exchange, 2009)
Salt Prayers (5/29 – 10/24/98) (published by The Ecstatic Exchange, 2005)
Some (10/25/98 – 4/25/99) (published by The Ecstatic Exchange, 2014)
Flight to Egypt (5/1 – 5/16/99)
I Imagine a Lion (5/21 – 11/15/99) (published by The Ecstatic Exchange, 2006)
Millennial Prognostications (11/25/99 – 2/2/2000) (published by The Ecstatic Exchange, 2009)
Shaking the Quicksilver Pool (2/4 – 10/8/2000) (published by The Ecstatic Exchange, 2009)
Blood Songs (10/9/2000 – 4/3/2001)(Published by The Ecstatic Exchange, 2012)
The Music Space (4/10 – 9/16/2001) (published by The Ecstatic Exchange, 2007)
Where Death Goes (9/20/2001 – 5/1/2002) (published by The Ecstatic Exchange, 2009)
The Flame of Transformation Turns to Light (99 Ghazals Written in English) (5/14 – 8/21/2002) (published by The Ecstatic Exchange, 2007)
Through Rose-Colored Glasses (7/22/2002 – 1/15/2003) (published by The Ecstatic Exchange, 2007)
Psalms for the Broken-Hearted (1/22 – 5/25/2003) (published by The Ecstatic Exchange, 2006)
Hoopoe's Argument (5/27 – 9/18/03)
Love is a Letter Burning in a High Wind (9/21 – 11/6/2003) (published by The Ecstatic Exchange, 2006)
Laughing Buddha/Weeping Sufi (11/7/2003 – 1/10/2004) (published by The Ecstatic Exchange, 2005)
Mars and Beyond (1/20 – 3/29/2004) (published by The Ecstatic Exchange, 2005)

Underwater Galaxies (4/5 – 7/21/2004) (published by The Ecstatic Exchange, 2007)
Cooked Oranges (7/23/2004 – 1/24/2005 (published by The Ecstatic Exchange, 2007)
Holiday from the Perfect Crime (1/25 – 6/11/2005) (published by The Ecstatic Exchange, 2011)
Stories Too Fiery to Sing Too Watery to Whisper (6/13 – 10/24/2005) (published by The Ecstatic Exchange, 2014)
Coattails of the Saint (10/26/2005 – 5/10/2006) (published by The Ecstatic Exchange, 2006)
In the Realm of Neither (5/14/2006 – 11/12/06) (published by The Ecstatic Exchange, 2008)
Invention of the Wheel (11/13/06 – 6/10/07)(published by The Ecstatic Exchange, 2010)
The Sound of Geese Over the House (6/15 – 11/4/07)
The Fire Eater's Lunchbreak (11/11/07 – 5/19/2008) (published by The Ecstatic Exchange, 2008)
Sparks Off the Main Strike (5/24/2008 – 1/10/2009) (published by The Ecstatic Exchange, 2010)
Stretched Out on Amethysts (1/13 – 9/17/2009)(published by The Ecstatic Exchange, 2010)
The Throne Perpendicular to All that is Horizontal (9/18/09 – 1/25/10) (published by The Ecstatic Exchange, 2014)
In Constant Incandescence (2/10 – 8/13/10) (published by The Ecstatic Exchange, 2011)
The Caged Bear Spies the Angel (8/30/10 – 3/6/11) (published by The Ecstatic Exchange, 2010)
This Light Slants Upward (3/7 – 10/13/11)
Ramadan is Burnished Sunlight (part of This Light Slants Upward, published separately by The Ecstatic Exchange, 2011)
The Match That Becomes a Conflagration (10/14/11 – 5/9/12)
Down at the Deep End (5/10 – 8/3/12) (published by The Ecstatic Exchange, 2012)
Next Life (8/9/12 – 2/12/13) (published by The Ecstatic Exchange, 2013)

The Soul's Home (2/13 – 10/8/13) (published by The Ecstatic Exchange, 2014)
Eternity Shimmers & Time Holds its Breath (10/10/13 – 1/27/14) (published by The Ecstatic Exchange, 2014)
He Comes Running (part of Eternity Shimmers, published as an Ecstatic Exchange Chapbook, 2014)
The Sweet Enigma of it All (1/29 – 6/18/14) (published by The Ecstatic Exchange, 2014)
Let Me See Diamonds Everywhere I Look (6/18/14 –)